REMBRANDT

T&J

Published by TAJ Books International LLC 2014
5501 Kincross Lane
Charlotte, North Carolina, USA
28277

www.tajbooks.com
www.tajminibooks.com

 The Publisher wishes to thank Johnbod.

ISBN 978-1-84406-328-4
Paperback 978-1-62732-019-1

Printed in China

1 2 3 4 5 18 17 16 15 14

REMBRANDT

T&J

SANDRA FORTY

REMBRANDT

1606–1669

Rembrandt is indisputably the greatest artist of the 17th century, and many would say the greatest artist of all time. His mastery of composition, paint, and line—he was a superlative etcher—over a lifetime's work has rarely been emulated, let alone surpassed. At a time when other artists specialized, his themes covered history, pastoral and Biblical scenes, group paintings, and most celebrated of all, portraits. Surprisingly little is known about him personally because he had no contemporary biographer and left no personal writings. He lived his entire life in and around Leiden and Amsterdam—at the time the latter was the wealthiest and most important city in Europe; obviously, he felt no need to go elsewhere.

A master of every style or genre he employed, it was through his portraits that he became a very successful artist and, for a time, a wealthy man. Like his clients he loved exotic settings, rich colors, elaborate costumes, and good stories, but tastes change and in time his style became unfashionable. Although he maintained a prolific output, the later years of his life were marred by financial hardship as the Dutch economy took a downturn, artistic tastes moved on, and he overspent.

Throughout the span of his life, Rembrandt painted his own face numerous times—over 90 authenticated portraits exist—so we have a strong visual impression of how he looked as he progressed from a young man in the 1620s through adulthood until his death in 1669. These self-portraits are composed of roughly 50 paintings, 32 etchings, and seven drawings. Most are painted from the same angle, showing just his head and shoulders with his body slightly twisted toward the viewer and a jaunty hat atop his head. The mystery is why he painted himself so often. It is probably, however, that he was studying how to render facial expressions, as well as perpetuating his own image (after all his paintings and etchings sold well) so as to publicize his work and reinforce his reputation.

Rembrandt Harmenszoon van Rijn was born on July 15, 1606, the eighth child of nine, in the Dutch town of Leiden. His father, Harmen Gerritszoon van Rijn, was a comfortably prosperous miller, and his mother, Cornelia Neeltje Willemsdr. van Suijttbroeck, was the daughter of a baker. Rembrandt was the only child in his family to be sent to the Latin School; the others were all destined for trade. After childhood they disappear from Rembrandt's narrative, so possibly he lost touch with them when he moved to Amsterdam. At the Latin School he would have been taught the Bible, classical history, mythology, and Latin—all subjects he later

Self-Portrait at the Age of 63
1669, The National Gallery, London
86 x 70.5, Oil on canvas

explored in his paintings.

Around the age of 14, Rembrandt was sent to the University of Leiden, one of the most distinguished centers of learning in Europe. But he did not flourish in academia and within months he convinced his parents to allow him to apprentice himself to an artist so that he could become one himself. His parents undoubtedly would have been reluctant because his education had prepared him for a respectable profession. Nevertheless, his talent must have been so apparent that they conceded to his request. Unfortunately, none of his early works have survived so it is impossible to assess his very early skills.

Accordingly, in 1620 Rembrandt became apprenticed to the best local artist, Jacob Isaaxszoon van Swanenburgh, with whom he stayed for about three years. Hungry to learn more, he persuaded his father to allow him to go to Amsterdam to study with Pieter Lastman, a reknowned painter of that era who specialized in colorful and dramatic historical and mythological compositions. Presumably Rembrandt thought Lastman had little to impart as he only stayed for six months before returning home to set up his own studio as an independent artist.

Back in Leiden he shared a workshop with his close friend and fellow artist, Jan Lievens. Jan, too, had been sent to Amsterdam to study with Pieter Lastman, staying for two years. At the time they worked together, the two young artists employed a very similar style, especially their use of light and shadow–very much in Caravaggio's style–and their preference for grand, theatrical, exotic settings. They are thought to have collaborated in creating over 25 works comprising drawings, paintings, and etchings. They shared models and painted portraits of each other. Both young artists made a reputation for themselves as artists to watch. In later years, and perhaps even still, their paintings from this period have frequently been misattributed to the other.

In the past the Catholic Church had been the great patron of artists, but that changed with the Protestant Reformation. By the 17th century the Netherlands had thrown off its Spanish oppressors and grown into a wealthy mercantile country with a thriving middle class that appreciated and commissioned art from Dutch painters–especially portraits and family groupings.

At first, Rembrandt specialized in Biblical and historical figure paintings, principally of old men. These were successful, and when he was only 21, in February 1628, Rembrandt accepted his first pupil, Gerard Dou. One year later, Rembrandt was visited by the diplomat and scholar Constantijn Huygens, the personal secretary of Prince Frederik Henry of Orange. Huygens suggested Rembrandt and Lievens would both benefit from a visit to Italy to observe the artistic talent of that region.

The pair disagreed, arguing that the talent displayed in the Netherlands was more than sufficient to nurture their talent. Huygens wrote of the pair, "I venture to suggest offhand that Rembrandt is superior to Lievens in his sure touch and in the liveliness of emotion. Conversely, Lievens is the greater in inventiveness and audacious themes and forms." Huygens must have preferred Lievens because he invited him to visit The Hague to paint his portrait.

The partnership ended in 1631 when Lievens went to England, hoping to earn his living at the court of King Charles I, and when Rembrandt moved to Amsterdam. Since that time, Rembrandt overshadowed his friend, although both ended up widowed and poverty-stricken in Amsterdam at the end of their lives.

Rembrandt's first important portrait was commissioned in 1630-31 by Nicolaes Ruts (Plate 14), an Amsterdam merchant who earned his fortune trading with Russia, which explains the rich furs he is wearing in Rembrandt's portrait of him. Rembrandt was then 25 years old and a recognized rising star of the Dutch art world. Rembrandt and Hendrick van Uylenburgh, an influential Amsterdam art dealer, formed a mutually beneficial business partnership–van Uylenburgh would find and secure the clients and Rembrandt would paint their portraits. On his move to Amsterdam Rembrandt lodged in van Uylenburgh's home in Breestraat.

Van Uylenburgh ran an artists' workshop where clients could have their portraits painted as well as have their paintings restored or copied. Rembrandt joined the studio and with van Uylenburgh's backing rapidly became Amsterdam's leading portraitist. In the four years he was with van Uylenburgh, Rembrant produced around 50 (extant) portraits; perhaps others have been lost.

The group portrait was a traditional and conventional form of painting in the Netherlands that was used to commemorate and celebrate families, craft guilds, or groups of businessmen. They showed soberly dressed people sitting in formal rows or semi-circles, and the paintings were hung on meetinghouse walls and in homes of the wealthy. In this vein, Dr. Nicolaes Tulp, a celebrated Amsterdam physician, commissioned a large group portrait from Rembrandt. But when Rembrandt tackled the subject as in *The Anatomy Lesson of Dr. Nicolaes Tulp* (Plate 21), he changed the traditional rules, depicting an informally arranged group. This more informal style had never been attempted before, and by introducing it, Rembrandt revolutionized the composition of group portraits by giving each man individuality and personal energy.

A great deal of Rembrandt's output was

drawings and etchings, mostly done as studies or for his own amusement. With a few deceptively simple lines he could conjure anything he wanted. It was his etchings that won him an international reputation as a great artist during his own lifetime—not often an easy feat for an artist. His etchings show a spontaneity that no other artist has been able to achieve. His subject range was wide: landscapes, portraits, self-portraits, nudes, animals, Biblical scenes, pastoral idylls, and genre scenes. Rembrandt mastered them all with seeming ease.

International buyers were keen to acquire his etchings. It is recorded that even in the year he died—1669—a Sicilian nobleman bought 189 engravings from him. Of course, the beauty of engravings for an artist is that many prints can be made from the same plate. Some 290 of Rembrandt's published prints survive, for which about 79 original plates still exist, many of them quite small. Rembrandt revised his plates, sometimes over the period of a couple of years, pulling each subsequent version off the press; in his lifetime, collectors fought to buy each of the various editions of a particular print.

Hendrick van Uylenburgh had an attractive young cousin named Saskia. In 1633 Rembrandt and Saskia van Uylenburgh became engaged. His first portrait of her was a delicate silverpoint study showing her in a flower-decorated broad-rim straw hat smiling gently at him. Underneath the painting his inscription reads, "This was made when my wife was twenty-one years old, the third day after our betrothal—8th of June 1633."

They married the following year on July 22, in the parish church of St. Anna in Friesland when Rembrandt was 28 and Saskia 21. Rembrandt was marrying well above his social station. Saskia was from a patrician family in Leeuwarden where her father had been burgomaster. None of Rembrandt's family attended the wedding; the reason for this absence is not known. Saskia had been orphaned at the age of 12, being reared by her three older brothers and four older sisters. She brought with her to the marriage a sizeable dowry left by her parents.

At first the young couple lodged together with her uncle, but soon they moved to a rented house in fashionable Niewe Doelenstraat. Rembrandt painted Saskia a number of times, most notably in 1635 as *Saskia van Uylenburgh in Arcadian Costume* (Plate 36) when she was heavily pregnant with their first baby. In the painting she is presented as Flora, the goddess of spring. The baby was born in December 1635. He was christened Rumbartus, but died within two months. In July 1638, Saskia gave birth to Cornelia (named after Rembrandt's mother), but she too died, at only three weeks of age.

Yet another baby girl, also called Cornelia, born in July 1640, also died at the age of three weeks. Only the couple's last child, Titus, born on September 22, 1641, grew to adulthood, but sadly died when he was only 27 years old. Despite these awful tragedies, their marriage was happy judging by the tender portraits Rembrandt painted of Saskia, but it was inevitably scarred by loss.

Ironically, in the mid-1630s, at the same time that tragedy struck in his personal life, Rembrandt was experiencing great success in his professional life as a very popular portraitist. Although he charged a great deal for his services, he enjoyed a long waiting list from the city guilds and from important families not only as a portraitist but also as a tutor for aspiring young artists.

Rembrandt had become the most fashionable painter in all the Netherlands, not just Amsterdam. He took on a number of apprentices to help with his workload, a development that has led the authorship of some of his paintings to be thrown into doubt. A good example of this was provided in March 2014 when the British National Trust announced that the world's leading Rembrandt expert—Ernst van de Wetering, Dutch art historian and Chair of the Rembrandt Research Project (RRP)—had reattributed to Rembrandt a portrait that the RRP had concluded 40 years ago was produced by one of Rembrandt's pupils. This bombshell immediately elevated the value of the painting, now considered to be a self-portrait, to over £20 million.

Rembrandt's most famous painting from this period is the virtuoso *Belshazzar's Feast* (Plate 38). He got the Hebrew inscription from his Rabbi friend Menasseh ben Israel, whose portrait he etched in 1636, but arranged the wording incorrectly—it should read from right to left—and mistranscribed one of the characters.

With a bit of money behind him, both earned and from Saskia's dowry, Rembrandt became a reckless buyer of antiquities: interesting costumes, armor, weapons, and various objets d'art—anything that looked interesting and could be used as stage dressing for his compositions. He became so involved in this endeavor that Saskia's family worried he was throwing away her inheritance. To add fuel to the fire, Rembrandt and Saskia moved into a grand house on Sint Anthoniesbreestraat next door to van Uylenburgh; the house became a museum to Rembrandt in 1911.

Rembrandt was earning a very good living and was in demand both as a painter and a teacher, but his home life was about to fall apart. In 1640 his mother died. Just two years later on June 15, 1642, a few months before her 30th birthday, after being weakened by her last pregnancy, Saskia died. Just before her death, she wrote her will leaving everything to Rembrandt and Titus, but with a condition that Rembrandt would forfeit his share if he remarried. The official cause of her death was consumption, but she was probably a victim of tuberculosis or plague.

Rembrandt was left all alone with a young baby. To look after baby Titus, Rembrandt employed a widowed nurse called Geertge Dix and she soon became his mistress. But then Rembrandt fell in love with another of his servants, Hendrickje Stoffels, a woman some 20 years his junior, and he dismissed Dix. As the spurned woman, Dix took Rembrandt to court for breach of promise. He responded with charges that she stole and pawned some of Saskia's jewelry. Dix could not convince the judge of her innocence and was instead sent to a house of correction in Gouda where she was incarcerated for five years. Domestic life then finally settled down for Rembrandt, although he could not marry Stoffels for the loss of Saskia's money. Much to the despair of the church, they lived together as common-law husband and wife.

Rembrandt completed *Night Watch* (Plate 47) in 1642, the year Saskia died. Commissioned by the Cloveniers (musket bearers) Company in 1640 for the main hall of the Arquebusiers guild building, it was

Now part of the Rembrandt House Museum, the showroom and bed of the painter, at left.

Rembrandt's house in Amsterdam where he lived for nearly 20 years until 1656. It has been renovated to appear as it would when he lived there. Items in the house are similar to those he owned and was forced to auction in order to relieve his bankruptcy in 1656, the year he vacated the property. An adjacent building houses numerous Rembrandt etchings.

Rembrandt's largest work and originally titled *The Militia Company of District II under the Command of Captain Franz Banninck Cocq.* The painting showed the now ceremonial officers of the Watch marching out with Captain Banninck Cocq, swathed in black, accompanied by his lieutenant, Willem van Ruytenburgh, dressed in yellow. They are surrounded by 16 men from the company as well as a young girl–the company's mascot. The girl has a chicken hanging from her belt, its claws (*clauweniers*) a pun referring to the company's name, Cloveniers. She is also holding the company's ceremonial drinking horn. The shield above the gate shows the names of the 18 people who paid to be in the painting. Again Rembrandt broke convention by showing the participants in the process of doing something–not just standing still and posing. It gave the picture an unexpected dynamism.

Professionally, Rembrandt almost ceased portrait painting after 1640, although he did continue to paint himself, friends, and family. A number of his pupils were now taking the lion's share of commissioned portraiture. In lieu of portraits, he painted landscapes and less extravagant religious themes, perhaps seeking solace in prayer after much of the turmoil in his life. It is also possible that he may simply have become bored with the process of portraits–similar patrician patrons, in similar pose, and no doubt similar small talk. Art historians see this new, darker phase as his emotional response to the tragedy in his life. Rembrandt began to paint in broad strokes and often smeared on paint with a palette knife–all producing a much rougher but more vigorous finish than was expected. Many critics started to label his work as "crude" and unrefined in its execution.

After having lived beyond his means for most of his adult life, Rembrandt faced dire financial straits by the mid-1650s. He resorted to loans to pay his debts. Creditors eventually began to chase him and he started to sell off parts of his extensive collections. The only good personal news came in 1654 when Hendrickje gave birth to Cornelia (the name previously given to two of Rembrandt's short-lived baby daughters); she was the only one of his children to outlive him.

In 1656 Rembrandt's financial affairs were critical. In July of that year, he successfully applied for a *cessio bonorum* by which he avoided imprisonment and bankruptcy on condition that he sold everything he owned in honesty and of good faith. All his goods and paintings were sold for a fraction of their value in two auctions held in 1657 and 1658 and he, Hendrickje, and Titus moved to the other, poorer side of Amsterdam to lodgings in the cheap district on the Rozengracht. Coincidentally, his old friend Jan Lievens also ended up there, widowed and penniless. But he set up a studio and resumed painting at an astonishing rate—more Rembrandts are dated 1661 than any year since the early 1630s. For legal purposes Hendrickje and Titus became business partners and "employed" Rembrandt so that he could keep the money he earned. Many self-portraits date from his later years but despite his problems he still looks dignified and resourceful.

In the early 1660s, Hendrickje suffered from a lingering illness and died in 1663, leaving Rembrandt and Titus alone. Titus married Magdalena van Loo, the daughter of an old family friend, in 1668, but died seven months later, six months before the birth of his daughter, Titia, in March 1669.

In 1668 Rembrandt produced one of his greatest paintings, *Return of the Prodigal Son* (Plate 82), based on a story from the New Testament's gospel of Luke. In the center of the dark painting, the figures of father and son glow with light. This Biblical painting is infused with Rembrandt's power of realism, spiritual insight, and personal understanding of tragedy.

Rembrandt lived his last years in the company of his daughter, Cornelia, and Rebecca Willems, an old servant woman. He died on October 4, 1669, at the age of 63 and was buried with few mourners and little ceremony in the Westerkerk four days later, alongside Titus and Hendrickje. An inventory was made of his few remaining possessions, mostly household objects, but also some antiquities and 13 paintings. The paintings included *Return of the Prodigal Son.*

Rembrandt left a vast catalog of works and even to this day his authorship of a number of paintings is still disputed. Not all of the works are in good condition, and many of them have been "improved" by later artists, masking the original brushwork. Rembrandt's work was so influential that he was much imitated and copied, a practice that has unfortunately led to confusion about attribution. Now many of the paintings have been painstakingly cleaned so that the original colors and brushwork are readily apparent. Many of the paintings are not as dark as they once appeared, singing out with color after the removal of centuries of dirt and darkened varnish.

On June 15, 1985, Rembrandt's *Danae* (Plate 37), which had been created in 1636 and reworked 10 years later, was viciously attacked by a lunatic while it hung in the State Hermitage Museum in Moscow. Slashed twice with a knife and doused with acid, it was feared lost. Quick action on the part of the museum's restoration staff left 70 percent of the paint surface undamaged. After several years the restoration was accomplished and the restored painting was returned to its rightful place in the museum.

Plate 1

MUSICAL COMPANY

1626, Rijksmuseum, Amsterdam
63.5 x 48 cm, Oil on panel

TOBIT AND ANNA WITH THE KID

1626, Rijksmuseum, Amsterdam
39.5 x 30 cm, Oil on panel

REMBRANDT LAUGHING

c. 1628, The J. Paul Getty Museum, Los Angeles
22.2 x 17.1 cm, Oil on copper

SELF-PORTRAIT

c. 1628, Rijksmuseum, Amsterdam
22.6 x 18.7 cm, Oil on panel

Plate 5

PORTRAIT OF REMBRANDT WITH A GORGET

After c. 1629, Mauritshuis, The Hague, Netherlands
37.9 x 28.9 cm, Oil on panel

SELF-PORTRAIT, AGED 23

1629, Isabella Stewart Gardner Museum, Boston
89.7 x 73.5 cm, Oil on wood

Plate 7

THE LAUGHING MAN

1629–30, Mauritshuis, The Hague, Netherlands
15.3 x 12.2 cm, Oil on copper on panel

JEREMIAH LAMENTING THE DESTRUCTION OF JERUSALEM

1630, Rijksmuseum, Amsterdam
58 x 46 cm, Oil on panel

Plate 9

ANDROMEDA

c. 1630, Mauritshuis, The Hague, Netherlands
34 x 24.5 cm, Oil on panel

ANNA AND THE BLIND TOBIT

c. 1630, The National Gallery, London
63.8 x 47.7 cm, Oil on oak

Plate 11

SELF-PORTRAIT

1630, Nationalmuseum, Stockholm
15.5 x 12 cm, Oil on copper

AN OLD MAN IN MILITARY COSTUME

c. 1630–31, The J. Paul Getty Museum, Los Angeles
66 x 50.8 cm, Oil on panel

Plate 13

AN OLD WOMAN READING, PROBABLY THE PROPHETESS HANNAH

1631, Rijksmuseum, Amsterdam
60 x 48 cm, Oil on panel

NICOLAES RUTS

1631, The Frick Collection, New York City
116.8 x 87.3 cm, Oil on mahogany panel

Plate 15

OLD MAN WITH A GOLD CHAIN

1631, The Art Institute of Chicago
83.1 x 75.7 cm, Oil on panel

PORTRAIT OF A SCHOLAR

1631, The State Hermitage Museum, St. Petersburg, Russia
104.5 x 92 cm, Oil on canvas

Plate 17

SIMEON'S SONG OF PRAISE

1631, Mauritshuis, The Hague, Netherlands
60.9 x 47.9 cm, Oil on panel

THE ABDUCTION OF EUROPA

1632, The J. Paul Getty Museum, Los Angeles
64.6 x 78.7 cm, Oil on panel

Plate 19

ADORATION OF THE MAGI

1632, The State Hermitage Museum, St. Petersburg, Russia
45 x 39 cm, Oil on paper pasted on canvas

CHRIST IN THE STORM ON THE SEA OF GALILEE

1633, Stolen from the Isabella Steward Gardner Museum, Boston, on March 18, 1990
160 x 128 cm, Oil on canvas

Plate 21

THE ANATOMY LESSON OF DR. NICOLAES TULP

1632, Mauritshuis, The Hague, Netherlands
169.5 x 216.5 cm, Oil on canvas

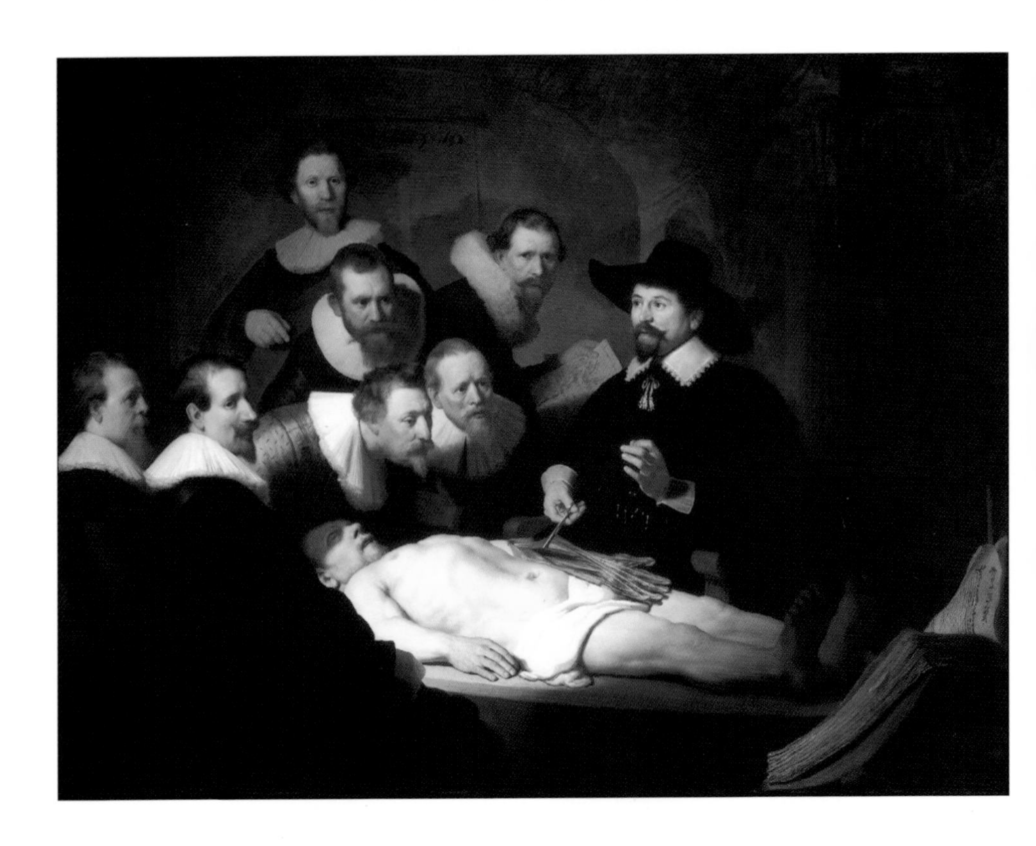

PORTRAIT OF JOHANNES WTENBOGAERT

1633, Rijksmuseum, Amsterdam
130 x 103 cm, Oil on canvas

Plate 23

JOSEPH TELLING HIS DREAMS TO HIS PARENTS AND BROTHERS

1633, Rijksmuseum, Amsterdam
51 x 39 cm, Oil on paper

ECCE HOMO

1634, The National Gallery, London
54.5 x 44.5 cm, Oil on paper mounted onto canvas

Plate 25

YOUNG WOMAN IN FANTASY COSTUME

1633, Rijksmuseum, Amsterdam
65 x 48 cm, Oil on panel

PORTRAIT OF HAESJE VAN CLEYBURGH

1634, Rijksmuseum, Amsterdam
68.6 x 53.4 cm, Oil on panel

DESCENT FROM THE CROSS

1634, The State Hermitage Museum, St. Petersburg, Russia
158 x 117 cm, Oil on canvas

FLORA

1634, The State Hermitage Museum, St. Petersburg, Russia
125 x 101 cm, Oil on canvas

PORTRAIT OF AECHJE CLAESDR.

1634, The National Gallery, London
71.1 x 55.9 cm, Oil on oak

PORTRAIT OF PHILIPS LUCASZ.

1635, The National Gallery, London
79.5 x 58.9 cm, Oil on oak

Plate 31

REMBRANDT AND SASKIA IN THE PARABLE OF THE PRODIGAL SON

c. 1635, Gemäldegalerie Alte Meister, Staatliche Kunstsammlungen Dresden
161 x 131 cm, Oil on canvas

SASKIA VAN UYLENBURGH, THE WIFE OF THE ARTIST

1634/35–1638/40, National Gallery of Art, Washington, DC
62.5 x 49 cm, Oil on panel

Plate 33

SACRIFICE OF ISAAC

1635, The State Hermitage Museum, St. Petersburg, Russia
193 x 132 cm, Oil on canvas

THE LAMENTATION OVER THE DEAD CHRIST

c. 1635, The National Gallery, London
31.9 x 26.7 cm, Oil on paper and pieces of canvas, mounted onto oak

MAN IN ORIENTAL DRESS

1635, Rijksmuseum, Amsterdam
72 x 54.5 cm, Oil on panel

SASKIA VAN UYLENBURGH IN ARCADIAN COSTUME

1635, The National Gallery, London
123.5 x 97.5 cm, Oil on canvas

Plate 37

DANAE

1636, The State Hermitage Museum, St. Petersburg, Russia
185 x 202.5 cm, Oil on canvas

BELSHAZZAR'S FEAST

c. 1636–38, The National Gallery, London
167.6 x 209.2 cm, Oil on canvas

Plate 39

A POLISH NOBLEMAN

1637, National Gallery of Art, Washington, DC
96.8 x 66 cm, Oil on panel

Plate 40

PARABLE OF THE LABOURERS IN THE VINEYARD

1637, The State Hermitage Museum, St. Petersburg, Russia
31 x 42 cm, Oil on panel

Plate 41

LANDSCAPE WITH A STONE BRIDGE

1638, Rijksmuseum, Amsterdam
29.5 x 42.5 cm, Oil on panel

STILL LIFE WITH PEACOCKS

c. 1639, Rijksmuseum, Amsterdam
145 x 135.5 cm, Oil on canvas

Plate 43

PORTRAIT OF A WOMAN, POSSIBLY MARIA TRIP

1639, Rijksmuseum, Amsterdam
107 x 82 cm, Oil on panel

SELF PORTRAIT AT THE AGE OF 34

1640, The National Gallery, London
102 x 80 cm, Oil on canvas

Plate 45

GIRL IN A PICTURE FRAME

1641, The Royal Castle in Warsaw Museum
105.5 x 76 cm, Oil on panel

DAVID AND JONATHAN

1642, The State Hermitage Museum, St. Petersburg, Russia
73 x 61.5 cm, Oil on panel

Plate 47

NIGHT WATCH

1642, Rijksmuseum, Amsterdam
379.5 x 453.5 cm, Oil on canvas

THE WOMAN TAKEN IN ADULTERY

1644, The National Gallery, London
83.8 x 65.4 cm, Oil on oak

HOLY FAMILY

1645, The State Hermitage Museum, St. Petersburg, Russia
117 x 91 cm, Oil on canvas

THE MILL

1645–48, National Gallery of Art, Washington, DC
87.6 x 105.6 cm, Oil on canvas

Plate 51

PORTRAIT OF A MAN, DR. EPHRAIM BUENO

1645–47, Rijksmuseum, Amsterdam
19 x 15 cm, Oil on panel

PORTRAIT OF AN OLD MAN IN RED

1652–54, The State Hermitage Museum, St. Petersburg, Russia
108 x 86 cm, Oil on canvas

THE KITCHEN MAID

1651, Nationalmuseum, Stockholm
78 x 64 cm, Oil on canvas

A WOMAN BATHING IN A STREAM (HENDRICKJE STOFFELS?)

1654, The National Gallery, London
61.8 x 47 cm, Oil on oak

Plate 55

PORTRAIT OF HENDRICKJE STOFFELS

Probably 1654–56, The National Gallery, London
101.9 x 83.7 cm, Oil on canvas

PORTRAIT OF AN OLD JEW

1654, The State Hermitage Museum, St. Petersburg, Russia
109 x 85 cm, Oil on canvas

Plate 57

A FRANCISCAN FRIAR

c. 1655, The National Gallery, London
89 x 66.5 cm, Oil on canvas

THE POLISH RIDER

c. 1655, The Frick Collection, New York City
116.8 x 134.9 cm, Oil on canvas

A WOMAN HOLDING A PINK

1656, National Gallery of Art, Washington, DC
103 x 86 cm, Oil on canvas

PORTRAIT OF A LADY WITH AN OSTRICH-FEATHER FAN

c. 1656–58, National Gallery of Art, Washington, DC
99.5 x 83 cm, Oil on canvas transferred to canvas

Plate 61

YOUNG WOMAN IN A DOORWAY

1656–57, Gemäldegalerie, National Museums Berlin
88.5 x 67 cm, Oil on canvas

YOUNG WOMAN WITH EARRINGS

1657, The State Hermitage Museum, St. Petersburg, Russia
39.5 x 32.5 cm, Oil on panel

Plate 63

A BEARDED MAN IN A CAP

Late 1650s, The National Gallery, London
78 x 66.7 cm, Oil on canvas

SELF-PORTRAIT

1658, The Frick Collection, New York City
133.7 x 103.8 cm, Oil on canvas

PHILEMON AND BAUCIS

1658, National Gallery of Art, Washington, DC
54.5 x 68.5 cm, Oil on panel transferred to panel

CHRIST AND THE SAMARITAN WOMAN

1659, The State Hermitage Museum, St. Petersburg, Russia
60 x 75 cm, Oil on canvas

AN ELDERLY MAN AS SAINT PAUL

1659, The National Gallery, London
102 x 85.5 cm, Oil on canvas

A YOUNG MAN SEATED AT A TABLE (POSSIBLY GOVAERT FLINCK)

c. 1660, National Gallery of Art, Washington, DC
109.9 x 89.5 cm, Oil on canvas

Plate 69

REMBRANDT'S SON TITUS IN A MONK'S HABIT

1660, Rijksmuseum, Amsterdam
79.5 x 67.7 cm, Oil on canvas

THE DENIAL OF ST. PETER

1660, Rijksmuseum, Amsterdam
154 x 169 cm, Oil on canvas

Plate 71

SELF-PORTRAIT AS THE APOSTLE PAUL

1661, Rijksmuseum, Amsterdam
91 x 77 cm, Oil on canvas

ST. BARTHOLOMEW

1661, The J. Paul Getty Museum, Los Angeles
86.7 x 75.6 cm, Oil on canvas

Plate 73

TWO MOORS

1661, Mauritshuis, The Hague, Netherlands
77.8 x 64.4 cm, Oil on canvas

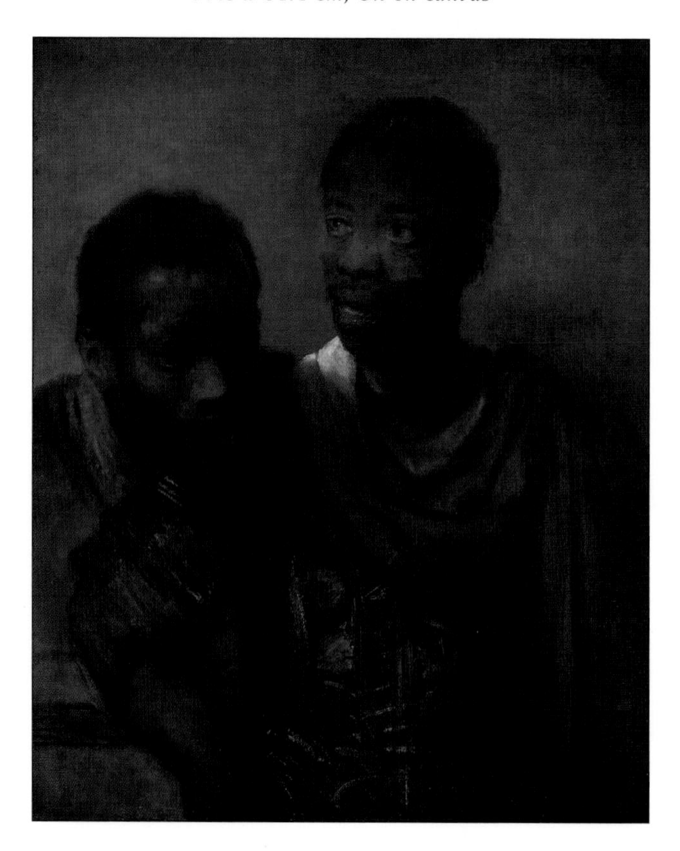

THE CONSPIRACY OF THE BATAVIANS UNDER CLAUDIUS CIVILIS

1662, Nationalmuseum, Stockholm
196 x 309 cm, Oil on canvas

Plate 75

THE WARDENS OF THE AMSTERDAM DRAPERS' GUILD (THE SYNDICS)

1662, Rijksmuseum, Amsterdam
191.5 x 279 cm, Oil on canvas

HOMER

1663, Mauritshuis, The Hague, Netherlands
107 x 82 cm, Oil on canvas

Plate 77

PORTRAIT OF FREDERICK RIHEL ON HORSEBACK

Probably 1663, The National Gallery, London
294.5 x 241 cm, Oil on canvas

LUCRETIA

1664, National Gallery of Art, Washington, DC
120 x 101 cm, Oil on canvas

Plate 79

HAMAN RECOGNIZES HIS FATE

c. 1665, The State Hermitage Museum, St. Petersburg, Russia
127 x 116 cm, Oil on canvas

ISAAC AND REBECCA (THE JEWISH BRIDE)

c. 1665–69, Rijksmuseum, Amsterdam
121.5 x 166.5 cm, Oil on canvas

Plate 81

PORTRAIT OF AN ELDERLY MAN

1667, Mauritshuis, The Hague, Netherlands
81.9 x 67.7 cm, Oil on canvas

RETURN OF THE PRODIGAL SON

c. 1668, The State Hermitage Museum, St. Petersburg, Russia
262 x 205 cm, Oil on canvas

INDEX